Moving AND Being

A collection of poems
shown in stillness

BY **PAMELA BRAY**

For David

who has the heart to encourage
and the courage to be truthful

© 2020 Pamela Bray All rights reserved.
No part may be reproduced or copied without the written consent of the author.
ISBN 978-0-6450110-0-5
Writing, book design and illustrations by Pamela Bray

Contents

Why?
Why Moving and Being?
About the Book and Me

Moving

Flight of Stillness 3
Heart and Mind 5
The Cycle Continues 6
Circle of Music 9
Together 11
A Very Small Island 13
Two as One 15
Awakened 17

Being

I've Come 21
The Taste of the Bell 23
Delight of Existence 24
From the Shadows 27
The Guardian 29
Still Flame 31
Shift 32
I Choose 34
Nothing 37
Fire and Water 38
The Space 41
I Wear Him 43

Why?

To scratch an itch.

To make physical that which is abstract.

To create.

Why Moving and Being?

For the past thirty years or so, these have been at the centre of my life.

The search for my life's purpose serendipitously led me to find like-being people,
a life's work with the breath, and a creative discipline with dance and movement as a way
of bringing stillness into my life, not just on the meditation cushion, but in every part of my life.

Some of these pieces date back to the nineties, some are inspired
by my work and experiences in the last five years but most are from now.

This book is really for me, but if you have happened upon it
I hope you may find some resonance with it, that you may recognise
something in yourself that only shows itself in the stillness.

About the Book and Me

I would not call myself a writer or a poet but I do write.

My path to this point has led me through 30ish careers, experiments, and hobbies (teaching and training, technical writing, marketing, photography, illustration, glass art and graphic design in all its forms including agency and corporate, books, calendars, CD packaging, ...) – all of these different, quite varied, some entered into for the right reasons, and some for the wrong. Invariably the greatest lessons are from the wrong. The one common thread is the creative.

In this case it's words and design.
With several writing projects at various stages of stuckness, I needed to complete something. I started simply with my most impactful experiences that were still real in me. From there, in a quiet space, the words and ideas flowed, often each piece was completed in a single sitting.

As their number grew, the designer in me kicked in, and I started the book design. While placing the poems, the idea for the series of illustrations took form. So for a while, as the poem was completed in the book, the illustration was following on immediately. Sometimes it just wasn't there, so I moved on. It would always reveal itself on return.

This collection feels true to me – at the moment – full of tenderness, richness and love.
I hope there is something here for you.

Pamela
2020

Moving

Flight of Stillness

The sacred, old wisdom connects the threads of the great unknown
As sweet delicate hands fashion them into the postures of the heart.
Her fluid form, graceful and gentle,
Weaves the music into and out of her awareness,
And, in rhythmic circles, she draws them to an expansive release.

She bows.
Fine feathered wings lift in flight
Creating spaces great and small.
A light touch to the ground
Connects her, prepares the way.
New pulsing wings push her upward,
Her left arm raised like a flying arrow –
Dynamic flight of stillness.

Heart and Mind

Heart and mind
Pulsing, surging, circling
As each foot searches for its right place,
Still, in a torrent of music.

In a beautiful tumbling to earth
I unfold and draw in
This awakening to an infinite realm,
Opening the circle of connection.

Arms will the music into being,
Exploring the space,
Massaging the movement,
As one, like an ocean.

With the delicate pulse of the heart
And the flame, still, in the eye of the storm
The notes slow.
I step back, note by note,
Hand on brow, hand on heart.

The Cycle Continues

Crystalline music flows over the feeling of water
Moving within the freedom.
Hands move, delicate and so fine,
Gesturing, searching, finding the throat
And waving with purpose, forward,
Leading the way.

The rhythmic beating of cosmic time
Synthesises the old and the new.
Tentatively the toe explores the space
As it learns to tap, and step beyond,
Defining its movement, balanced with grace,
Into the story of reconnection.

The balance of life is held intact.
The cycle continues, the space opens.
The narrow corridor holds the dance,
Holds the long steady movement,
Anticipating the move forward,
Majestic and simple and slow.

Light breaks. The melody explodes.
Feet of joy dance the rectangular pattern with dynamic majesty
As the body reaches and sweeps
Carrying hope, as the beauty is felt.

Notes cascade like heavenly water
Under the starry sky of the cosmos.
The majestic feminine dances her story
Of devotion, of creation, of life.
Come into me. Be one with me,
As the blending of the forces is focused.

Searching. In the dark.
Sensing. Exploring. Playing.
Balancing. The mystery and the journey.
Awakening. A new world. An exquisite heart.
Experiencing. The unknown emotion. The complete reverence.
The cycle completes, to begin again.

Circle of Music

Within the circle
All is contained.
Tumultuous music rains down –
A torrent of resonant sound,
A riffing melody,
Building, repeating.

The slow beat belies the multitude of notes
That massage the moment,
Expanding the vibrations that tumble into her body
And gather at her feet.

The circle bursts opens
Spilling the lifeforce of its melody in freeform ripples,
Their pattern, an embodiment of her longing
To explore freedom.

They were moved.
For him – a body in *his* body, a melody previously stillborn.
For her – gentle hands at her back, and the demand of many planes of existence.
The process of connection had begun.

They moved,
Feeling their way in the unknown.
The swelling strength,
The sensual feminine
Forming on pure hearts.

A single note
A joyful skip
The way is open, the spirit awakened.
The body plays with the freedom of shapes,
Fluttering its extremities,
Exploring its touch.
The simple joys of the fairy lightness
Held in pure balance
Till the final note.

A Very Small Island

I flounder,

My limbs awkward in their movement.

The coarseness and the heaviness

Belie the fluid motion in my mind.

I see her and I feel her within me.

She has no weight,

Just a fine veil moving to the breeze of the music.

There is no separation between them –

The form is the rhythm

The notes are the dance.

I release into the music.

Feel it, not hear it.

Let it beat my heart, pulse my blood,

Entice my being into its passionate play.

I am now the music.

I am now the dance.

Two as one, swirling in ascending arcs

But hushed in the stillness –

A very small island in a vast ocean of sound.

Two as One

Two as one
Blended yet separate
Whole and complete
In their union and in themselves –
One giving to the other and one open, receptive –
Their wish to be the silent flame.

Essence, soul, spirit –
All a blending
Of unique radiant colours,
Unfolding mysterious entwining paths –
A blossoming here and now
Uncovered in the search for truth
In an emerging expression of love.

Awakened

I step softly, feeling the next move.
I look up, lean forward, intensity in my gaze.
Everything drops away in a spiraling plunge,
My feet at the edge... of nothing.
Fear rises. It sways my body, windmills my arms,
Lifts me, leaves me balancing.

The tumultuous sound of the ocean waves press into my space.
My heart pulsing, my body upright,
My arms now outstretched, my gaze upward –
I am connected to a mystery,
Awakened into a new world.

I search this world, face lifted and alive,
Eyes closed, sensing in the dark,
Its rich expression, the real connection.
I sense another self, not present.
I breathe in, and step forward into the openness.

Being

I've Come

I've come

I walk to the edge of the dawn imminent
Still
no breath
darkest of dark.

There... a brilliant speck
There... a pinhole in the dark...
light rushing through,
gaining strength
to star-like brilliance.

Suddenly the dark tears apart
and the light pours through
in the most delicate of hues –
colours new-born in the pristine stillness, in this pure space.

They lay on each other – these colours – melding their hues like lovers.

The Taste of the Bell

Eyes bright, ears keen, touch acute.
Each playing their role in your life.

What if your eyes could taste? Your ears could smell? Your nose could hear?
What would the sky taste like? How would the dog's bark feel?
Could you *see* a whisper of wind? The *smell* of a cry? The *whimper* of the moon?
And what of the texture of blue? The taste of the bell?

Decouple the patterns of your senses,
Be awake, dynamic, receptive, available.
This is artist as creator.
Open to the un-norm, to the offbeat, to the unexpected,
To things that surprise and delight, that take the breath away.
Open to that unique view… of life, of thought, of form.

Open to a new way.

Delight of Existence

Seven points turn, wrinkling the deep purple satin of night.
One long arm stretches into the sky
Pouring the fabric of energy
Over the orb of life in angled spirals.
She gazes at the fall, serpentine tresses entwining her body,
Spilling at her feet into the crystal pattern –
The stars ignite a bright reflection in each facet.

By day he crashes through the waves of life,
Golden orb rays spill over his path.
Powerful soul wings beat him forward.
They curl and arc, translucent in their flight.
His arms reach forward, but just out of reach of the prize he seeks.
His body bent, tight, strained.
He follows instincts, great emotions, desires.

What is flowering here? Magic in the blossoming of this beauty?
Such differences, yet rich and strong in their feelings.
Such similarities in the fruit they bear.
The flow and the flowing of shared realisation, of the delight of existence, of happiness –
She under her star, he under the golden orb,
Sharing the joy, halving the sorrow,
Dual courage for that first unconventional dance –
His ancient instinct, her beautiful truth.

From the Shadows

Don't step into the shadows
hiding, unseen.

I am here.
I see you – see you hiding.

You think I don't care
because I don't come to you, can't come to you
in the shadows.
But I love you, my heart aches to help you,
but I can't help you there.

I wish, and I pray, that you feel my love
Tempting you back into my warmth.
Fall into the envelope of my love.
Feel it completely and rest in release.

The Guardian

His hands are like jewels.
His feet bear the wings of truth.
A flame burns in the solitude of his mind.
He holds the balance of life, intact,
The silence in the fire of his will
The stillness in the water of his heart.

He is the glow in the darkness
The golden light reaching for you,
Shining upon you, showing the way,
Giving hope.

Now is the perfect time.
Feel him, the simplicity of his touch,
The power of his presence, in waves of awareness.
Don't fear the smallness of life,
The vastness of that deep unknown.
See your truth, feel your colour,
Be the love.
Step.

Still Flame

I am the still flame,
The flickering flame,
The dual flame reflected.

My form is bound, but reaching.
Its fineness expanding upward,
Translucent, alive.
Its direction strong.

I am pure light.
Pure love.

Shift

Alone.
This plane of my life plays out.
I walk amongst it, through it,
But I am not there.
I am not seen, don't fit.
I walk another plane, laid bare.
Separate.

Today
I do not wish to belong,
Sad at not being needed, not included,
Unable to ask and chance rejection.
I am not deluded.
To walk away is my heart's protection,
But in pain.

Change
Creeping, hidden, subtle.
Clarity of thought and feeling and needs
Paralysed by confronting the fear –
The romance gone, just a garden of weeds.
With different eyes at the stark reality, I peer.
Shock.

Now
I must walk a truer path, an honest path,
Not one expected, not one of fear, not automatic.
Be clean, give fully each moment.
Release from the judgement and mind erratic,
To enough self – whole and comfortable – unbent.
Open.

I Choose

I flow
But do I grow
In this life's stream
Blessed by abundance, time to dream,
Its gentle current, its pace calm?
I do not veer, or risk harm.

Barriers, large and small, arise
Unwelcome, to my eyes.
I am affronted, fear the change.
I weather the new, in pain
Until I, again, find my flow
And settle in to comfort I know.

I see the flow with dismay
I cannot continue in this guarded way.
I plant my feet on the river bed
And look to the divided streams ahead.
I see the familiar flow.
Settled in, I do not grow.

Now I clearly see my course.
I cannot continue without remorse.
My feet I lift from the river floor,
My eyes the divided streams explore.
The familiar I clearly see
But it's the alternative that speaks to me.

Questions my heart can't refute
Of courage needed to be resolute.
To swim and not to glide
To sense and then decide.
To allow for truth, and not misuse
My life. I choose.

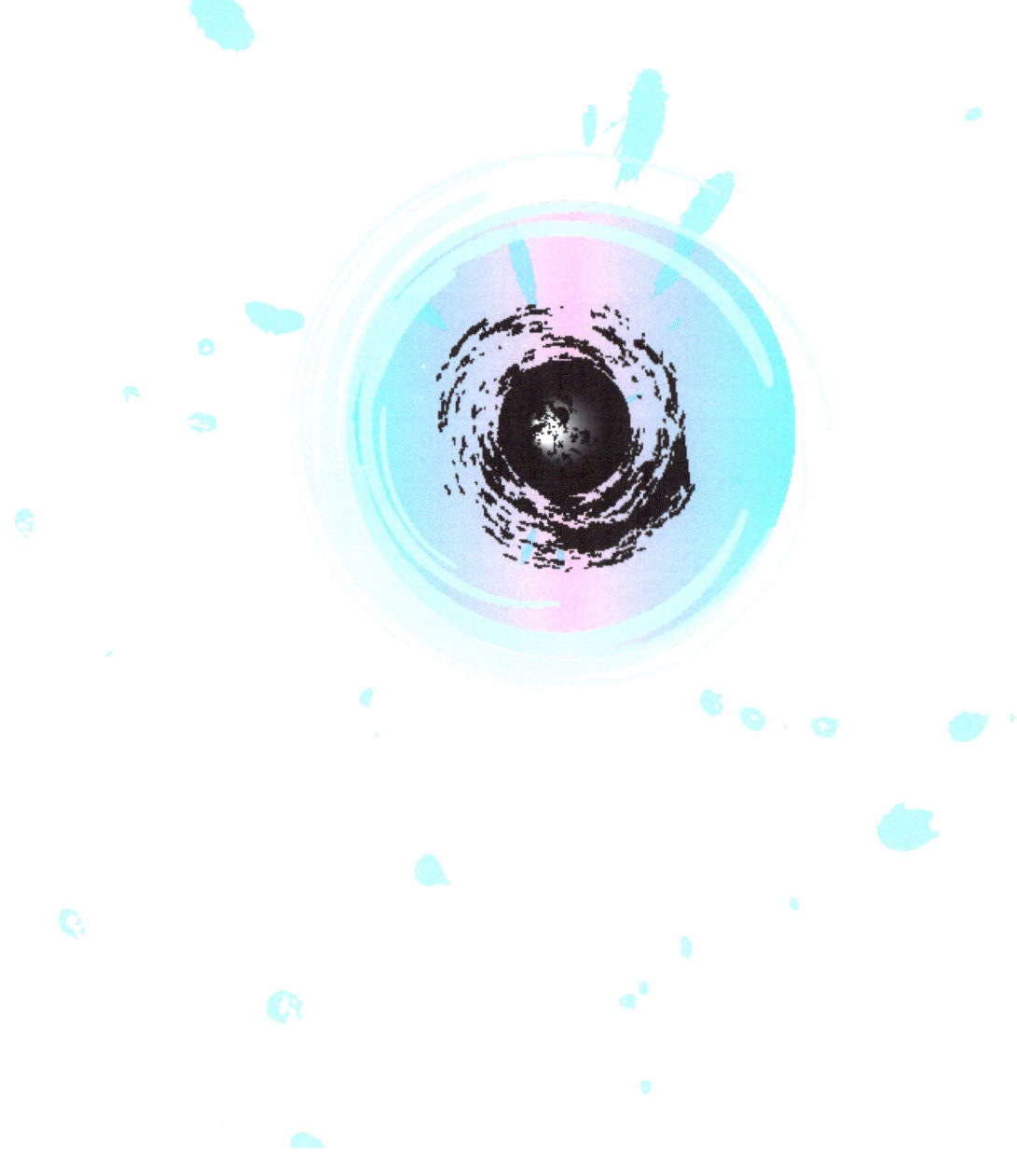

Nothing

Soul floating – all is stripped away.
Nothing left.

Sensation. Melting. Dissolving. Separation.
In my body but looking on. I am nothing.

Change the rhythm, and... now... something is possible.
Allow it to grow, eyes as windows, mind still.

Seeing, not looking. Listening, not hearing.
Waves of awareness replenish me.

Body humming – washed in awareness.
Enticed by all.

Alive. Engaged. Intense.
In my body and looking on. Connected with everything.

Fire and Water

She was born in the time of Fire and Water. A prosperous time for her people.
A time of power, a time where ceremony was all.
And she was born in this time, born of the two.
She was not to understand what this would mean to her, what her joining would be,
How different and dangerous was her path.
For now, she was just the bright star, the golden diamond in the heart of the two –
The fiery water, the rippling flame.

She was the centre, she surrounded all.
And her life was blessed.

The elaborate symbolism was read and reread.
She learned the way, and she stepped the path that was hers alone.
She did not falter but glowed in the fire and bathed in the water of her life.

At eighteen she gathered her final wand – the ninth - the complete set.
Each wand a milestone, an accomplishment, a learning.
They completed her expansion – her link to the fiery sun –
She, the arrow come from the half moon.

Her wands bore the moon's tips, the finest silvery emotional energy, their shafts the red of the fire,
And each end carried nine moons, one for each cycle of her life here.
These in their completeness, the bridge between moon and sun, kept all from the looming darkness,
Let them ride free of the harm that was all around them.
She was their guide. She was their light, by day and by night.
Her strength would be their strength.

The darkness passed.
The light returned, and all around were the brilliant reds and golds of this most celebrated day.
The transformation was complete.
Fire and water were one – a great swirling wave of fire curled and stretched upward,
Its energy lifting all who were near, bending the forms to its beautiful shape.

And, leading this upward rising, was The Grace,
Her newly formed wand – golden rod and golden sun – in her hand.
Her purity of form, naked in its simplicity, surrendering into the wave of fire,
Upwards – ever upwards – to complete her destiny.

They watched from the tower, their eyes unwavering.
Even in the heat of the fire all around,
This was her moment – their moment –
Shared.

The Space

Fill the space. Fill it full, tight.
Leave no space.
Allow the pain, the fight.
Kill the space.
Shroud the fear, sealed from light.

I walk the path worn by time. I know its way, I feel the climb.
I take each step, I know the way.
I do not turn, I do not sway.
All around are things to see – yet invisible to me.
I am blind on the path. I cannot open to see the spark.

I walk the path, new this time. I know the way, I sing its rhyme.
My step is light, I do not fear.
I wander along, so much to hear.
I feel my skin, I feel the air. I feel so calm, I am laid bare.
I am part of all I see. I feel the spark, I now can be.

Feel the space. Feel it full, bright.
Let be the space.
Allow its calm, its light.
Feed the space.
Feel no fear. Step. Take flight.

I Wear Him

I wear him like a blessing.

Seen
unexpectedly through other's eyes,
a snapshot, an expression.

Felt
more often, as an attitude, a posture, a talent.

Heard
with the outburst of a slapstick roar
or quietly in some cheeky humour.

Touched by memories:
held still in safety in the surf's waves
sun soaked skin on hot sand
the life of the party
the positive spin on life…

A life that now has slipped through the veil…
but I wear him as a blessing.